IZZ STRADLIN

The Quiet One Who Rocked the Loudest

Lucas Olen

TABLE OF CONTENT

INTRODUCTION

INTRODUCTION

The name Izzy Stradlin is ingrained in rock history. Jeffrey Dean Isbell was born in Lafayette, Indiana, on April 8, 1962. Stradlin's achievements as a founding member of Guns N' Roses, one of the most recognizable and significant rock bands ever, helped define a musical epoch that has remained relevant for decades. Izzy's distinctive rhythm guitar technique, quiet yet captivating demeanor, and outstanding songwriting greatly influenced the band's sound and popularity. His rise from a small-town childhood to international fame is a testament to his fortitude, artistic ability, and unwavering determination to follow his creative inclinations.

Stradlin's early years were enmeshed in the modest rhythms of small-town life while growing up in the Midwest. From an early age, he showed a rebellious side and a love of music, influenced by the raw energy of the rock and punk bands of the time as well as his grandmother's drumming skills. Izzy's love of music, which would eventually serve as the cornerstone of his career, was evident throughout his early years. He relocated to Los Angeles, a metropolis teeming with the aspirations of many budding musicians, after graduating from high school, with the goal of making a name for himself in the emerging rock scene.

The Sunset Strip in the 1980s was a fruitful environment where Izzy met other young, eager musicians who shared his ideas. Axl Rose, a Lafayette boyhood buddy who would go on to become the charismatic and controversial leader of Guns N' Roses, was one of them. Together, they established the foundation for a force that would shake the music industry. Guns N' Roses was formed with Slash,

Duff McKagan, and Steven Adler. They combined hard rock, blues, and punk elements to create a sound as unrefined and unrepentant as the streets they walked.

Often referred to as the glue that linked the band's many inspirations together, Stradlin played a crucial contribution. Izzy was largely responsible for the creative backbone, even though the attention was usually drawn to Slash's guitar prowess and Axl's erratic personality. His ability to create gritty, emotionally charged songs and his sense of rhythm were essential components of the band's identity. Songs such as "Patience," "Mr. His distinctive mark may be heard in "Brownstone" and "Double Talkin' Jive," which demonstrate his ability to combine melody with a hint of edge that reflected the erratic, chaotic energy of their life.

The 1987 publication of Guns N' Roses' debut album, Appetite for Destruction, launched the band into prominence. Fueled by singles like "Sweet Child O' Mine," "Welcome to the Jungle," and "Paradise City," the album solidified their position in rock history while capturing the unadulterated, rebellious spirit of a generation. Izzy's talents as a guitarist and songwriter were essential to the album's success, and his quiet composure served as a counterpoint to his comrades' exaggerated egos.

The demands of the rock-and-roll lifestyle started to wear them down despite their quick ascent to popularity. The commotion and excess that surrounded the band made Stradlin, who had always cherished his solitude and creative independence, feel more and more disillusioned. Izzy decided to leave Guns N' Roses in 1991, while they were at the top of their game. Fans and industry insiders were taken aback by the change, but it also demonstrated his dedication to being loyal to his creativity and personality.

With his departure from the band, Stradlin embarked on a new chapter in his career, one in which he would follow his own artistic path. With a focus on authenticity over commercial appeal, he recorded a number of albums as a solo artist that highlighted his passion for rock, blues, and roots music. Despite being less well-known than his Guns N' Roses days, he still had a devoted fan base and was respected for his honesty as a musician thanks to his solo efforts.

Over the years, Izzy Stradlin's attraction has only grown due to his mysterious personality. He has kept a quiet profile and let his music do the talking, preferring to avoid the spotlight. Even though he has occasionally performed with his old colleagues, like during Guns N' Roses' much anticipated reunion tour,

Stradlin maintains his independence and is motivated by his love of music rather than the perks of celebrity.

The impact of Izzy Stradlin goes well beyond his time with Guns N' Roses. His contributions to the rock music industry are proof of the strength of unadulterated skill, sincerity, and an unwavering dedication to one's artistic vision. He has made a lasting impression on music history with his lyrics, guitar playing, and understated charm. Izzy Stradlin's life and career are explored in this biography, which follows his rise from humble origins to rock stardom and examines the lasting influence of his work on both fans and other artists.

Chapter 1

Early Years and Their Impact

Born Jeffrey Dean Isbell on April 8, 1962, in Lafayette, Indiana, Izzy Stradlin grew up in a tiny Midwestern town with straightforward but influential rhythms. His early years were characterized by a strong sense of humility and work ethic, which served as the foundation for a character that would maintain its groundedness even in the face of eventual celebrity. Izzy first developed the raw edge and tenacity that would eventually characterize his music career in Lafayette, a town renowned for its sense of community and work ethic. Although his childhood was modest, it set the groundwork for the rebellious and imaginative attitude that would eventually motivate him.

Izzy's family life was complicated yet supportive at the same time. His mother worked in the telecommunications sector, while his father was an engraver. Both of them had steady, diligent careers. However, a pivotal point in Izzy's life was their divorce when he was still a small boy. Izzy took comfort in his friends' company and the expanding impact of music in spite of the difficulties this presented. His attitude on life and art would eventually be significantly influenced by the sense of freedom he developed during these early years.

Izzy grew up with pals who were as passionate about music and mischief as he was. Teenage rebellion frequently took place on Lafayette's peaceful streets, with bicycles and skateboards acting as means of escape and discovery. Izzy's pals exposed him to a variety of musical styles, sparking an interest that soon developed into a passion. He started to dream of a life outside of his little village during these formative years, one that would be influenced by creativity and music.

Izzy discovered music as a source of expression and a passion. It was a simple instrument, but his first guitar would be the beginning of a lifetime of self-expression. Izzy started training himself to play after being inspired by the sounds of the radio and the records whirring in neighborhood stores. He was captivated by the idea that music could express both passion and revolt in equal measure. His creative process was characterized by a tension between the complex feelings he found in the music of the moment and the simplicity of his surroundings.

The sources of inspiration for Izzy were as varied as they were significant. Punk rock struck a strong chord with his rebellious nature because of its unadulterated energy and uncompromising attitude. His adolescence was accompanied by bands like the Ramones and the Sex Pistols, which promoted uniqueness and nonconformity. At the same time, the Rolling Stones and Keith Richards, two legendary figures in classic rock, offered a model for fusing roughness with melody. Izzy's songwriting approach would subsequently be characterized by the fusion of these inspirations, which combined the timeless qualities of rock with the immediacy of punk.

Izzy's passion for music grew inextricably linked to who he was as he developed his abilities. He began performing in neighborhood bands, experimenting with various genres and sounds as he honed his own musical voice. These formative encounters were essential because they gave Lafayette a sense of direction and a window onto the outside world. He started to understand the ability of music to inspire, provoke, and connect at this period.

Izzy's transformation from an Indiana kid from a little town to a potential rock star was characterized by a combination of tenacity, inventiveness, and fortitude. His formative years, which were influenced by friends, family, and the many genres of punk and classic rock, served as evidence of how modest beginnings can spur enormous ambition. Izzy Stradlin's journey, which would soon alter the course of rock & roll, started in Lafayette, despite the city's remoteness from the glamour and mayhem of the music business.

Chapter 2

The Road to Guns N' Roses

Izzy Stradlin made the audacious choice to leave behind the comforts of Lafayette, Indiana, in favor of the chaotic potential of Los Angeles, which marked the beginning of the band Guns N' Roses. Los Angeles in the early 1980s was a draw for a young musician hoping to pursue a career in rock and roll. With its vibrant atmosphere, the Sunset Strip provided an opportunity to network, hone talents, and get fully immersed in the music industry. Izzy had a definite objective when she came to the city, despite having few belongings. The change from the peaceful streets of Lafayette to the expansive city was both thrilling and difficult. Grit was necessary for the unpredictability of big-city living, but Izzy was a good fit for the grind because of his quiet resolve and flexible personality.

At first, Los Angeles was not a glamorous place to live. Izzy focused on his music while doing odd jobs to support himself. As he looked for his musical identity, he played in a number of bands, experimenting with different sounds and approaches. These formative years taught him not just the ins and outs of the profession but also the tenacity required to thrive in it. Izzy persisted despite the difficulties because he thought that music was his calling.

Izzy reconnected with his Lafayette boyhood buddy Axl Rose in Los Angeles. A common love of music and a spirit of defiance had brought them together years before. Axl was a kindred soul with his charismatic demeanor and unadulterated singing ability. The chance meeting of two driven artists with complementing skills led to their accidental reunion. They both had lofty goals when they arrived in Los Angeles, and their reunion sparked a new creative flame. They started working together to create the foundation for what would grow to be one of the most recognizable bands in rock history.

Their initial days of working together were characterized by a spirit of exploration and friendship. They were inspired by blues, punk, and classic rock and had a profound love for music that cut beyond genres. Axl's blazing passion was counterbalanced by Izzy's easygoing manner and musical prowess, forming a combination that would characterize their collaboration. During this time, the two performed in a number of bands, but their discontent with the constraints of those endeavors inspired them to dream of something more ambitious. They believed that the scene lacked the raw energy and attitude, so they set out to establish a band that reflected those qualities.
When Izzy and Axl met other artists who shared their drive and desire for

success, their vision started to take shape. They gradually put together a lineup that embodied their musical philosophies. The band was complete with drummer Steven Adler, bassist Duff McKagan, and guitarist Slash. The band's sound was gritty, strong, and distinctly their own since each member contributed their own distinct flavor. Their shared sense of purpose and determination to push limits fostered their instant connection.

A combination of identities led to the band's name, Guns N' Roses. It mirrored the combination of vulnerability and ferocity that characterized their music. They rejected convention and adopted a lifestyle that reflected the rawness of their lyrics, being shamelessly themselves from the beginning. They stand out from the polished artists who dominate the charts because of their music, which combines the boldness of punk, the swagger of rock, and the soulfulness of blues. Fans connected with Guns N' Roses because they were a band that was gritty at times.

Their ascent was far from straightforward. The band gained a reputation for their thrilling live performances while playing tiny venues around the Sunset Strip. They produced erratic, powerful, and memorable sets; they were a turbulent force. As soon as word got out about their abilities, record labels began to take notice. Their genuineness and indisputable brilliance made them unavoidable despite the difficulties of navigating the profession.

Izzy saw the creation of Guns N' Roses as the result of years of perseverance, sacrifice, and hard labor. He played a crucial part in the band, providing stability in the middle of the mayhem. He made a substantial contribution to their early work as a songwriter, bringing his own style and viewpoint to their songs. His capacity to transform his feelings and experiences into music gave their compositions an unvarnished honesty that listeners found compelling.

Guns N' Roses had already made a name for themselves as a band to watch by the time they inked their first record deal. Appetite for Destruction, their debut album, was born out of the blood, sweat, and tears of their early days and would go on to reinvent the rock genre. Izzy saw this as the fulfillment of a dream that had started in Lafayette years prior, and it went beyond simple success. His trip to Los Angeles, his reunion with Axl, and the formation of Guns N' Roses were all significant components that contributed to the legacy of one of the most illustrious bands in rock history.

Chapter 3

The Making of a Rock Icon

The release of Guns N' Roses' debut album, Appetite for Destruction, which would go on to revolutionize rock music, cemented Izzy Stradlin's ascent to fame in the genre. Izzy's hands were all over the 1987 record, which encapsulated the unadulterated energy and irreverent attitude of a generation. His efforts as a lyricist were essential in determining the tone and plot of the album. Izzy was skilled at transforming personal experiences into lyrics that connected with listeners. His subtle yet moving compositional style gave the band's music a more genuine feel, distinguishing it from the glam rock and highly polished sounds that were popular at the time.

Like the band itself, the creative process for Appetite for Destruction was erratic and chaotic. The band members' hardships, aspirations, and excesses were reflected in the songs, which were inspired by their own experiences. Izzy had a key role in transforming these unfiltered feelings into approachable and thrilling music. Songs like "Mr. Brownstone," which Izzy and Slash co-wrote, explored the more sinister aspects of addiction by fusing a catchy beat with brutally honest lyrics. A key component of the album's popularity was his ability to capture the gritty aspects of their way of life while yet retaining a feeling of melody.

Izzy frequently relied on instinct to guide her artistic process. Izzy wanted to let the music do the talking rather than relying on flamboyance and show, as some of his comrades did. He frequently developed chord progressions and riffs on his guitar, which served as the basis for some of the band's most well-known songs. His ability to collaborate made it easy for him to work with the other members of the group, offering suggestions that would eventually become classic successes. The band's combined creativity was on full display in songs like "Sweet Child O' Mine" and "Paradise City," but Izzy's steadying influence was frequently what kept the creative process on course.

In addition to creating songs, Izzy's work on the rhythm guitar was essential to the band's style. He gave the tunes a constant, powerful foundation that let Slash's lead guitar shine. This harmony between lead and rhythm produced a dynamic that came to represent Guns N' Roses. Izzy's playing, which was based on rhythm and simplicity, gave the song an edge that was hard to ignore. Although he never sought attention, his influence could be heard in every rhythm and chord.

The band's life became a blur of shows, publicity, and extravagance as they embarked on a tour to promote Appetite for Destruction. They went from relative obscurity to international prominence thanks to the album's spectacular success, and the rigors of touring put their fortitude to the test. It was both thrilling and overwhelming for Izzy to go from being a struggling musician to an international rock sensation. The band was frequently pushed to its limits by their demanding schedule and the hedonistic lifestyle for which they were renowned. Izzy managed the highs and lows of their newfound success by staying focused on the music in spite of the mayhem.

There were two sides to life on the road. On the one hand, it made it possible for Guns N' Roses to engage with their audience on a visceral level and give unvarnished, intense, and memorable shows. However, it also made them aware of the negative aspects of success, where disputes and temptations may stop them in their tracks. Izzy frequently kept his distance from the drama, even if he was not immune to the excesses of the period. He stood out due to his more reserved nature, and he enjoyed his alone time more than the band's nonstop party vibe.

Appetite for Destruction achieved remarkable success. The album's raw depiction of Los Angeles life resonated with listeners worldwide, and songs like "Welcome to the Jungle" became anthems for a generation. It was the attitude that struck a chord, not simply the music. Izzy had a significant role in creating the rebellious persona that Guns N' Roses espoused. Izzy's quiet power and inventive talents were the glue that kept everything together, even if Slash's famous solos and Axl Rose's stage persona garnered most of the attention.

The band's ascent to stardom presented both possibilities and difficulties. They shattered records, played to packed venues, and came to represent rock's timeless appeal. However, challenges that questioned their unity accompanied their triumph. They started to feel the effects of their increasing fame and the unrelenting pace of touring. Ever the realist, Izzy saw the band's internal divisions. Even when the world around them became more chaotic, he stood out for his ability to take a step back and evaluate circumstances with objectivity.

It is impossible to overestimate Izzy Stradlin's contribution to the creation of Appetite for Destruction and the band's explosive success. He was a musician whose contributions were as significant as they were subtle, the calm hand in the middle of the storm. Guns N' Roses' reputation was greatly influenced by his songwriting, rhythm guitar skills, and unwavering commitment to the art form.

Izzy stayed loyal to himself and prioritized the music over the gimmicks of celebrity as the band's popularity soared. Because of his genuineness, he became not just a band member but also a rock star in his own right.

Chapter 4

The Core Songwriter

Izzy Stradlin, a fundamental composer whose subtle genius formed a pillar of the band's identity, was the silent driver behind a large portion of Guns N' Roses' success. Izzy's steady hand and talent for composing supplied much of the band's creative basis, even if the attention was frequently on Axl Rose's flashy appearance or Slash's explosive solos. In addition to shaping the band's style, his work with Axl and the rest of the band created some of the most recognizable songs of their time, inspiring a generation of rock fans who looked to their music for rebellion and comfort.

Axl Rose and Izzy worked together as complementing opposites. Izzy was a grounded artist who appreciated honesty and simplicity, in contrast to Axl, who was a theatrical vocalist with a taste for drama and intensity. Their partnership had a special depth because of their common past, which dates back to their adolescent years in Lafayette, Indiana. They respected one another and were able to push limits since they recognized one other's creative tendencies. Together, they combined Axl's narrative lyricism with Izzy's melodic skills to create songs that struck a balance between unadulterated emotion and structure. Songs like "Welcome to the Jungle" and "Sweet Child O' Mine" demonstrated this synergy and became classics that had an impact much beyond the Sunset Strip.

Izzy's ability to convey the essence of life's setbacks and victories in a way that seemed both intensely personal and broadly relevant defined his vocation as a composer. His contributions, which frequently reflected themes of addiction, relationships, and the harsh reality of living on the edge, were frequently based on his personal experiences. Among his greatest accomplishments, "Mr. Co-written with Slash, "Brownstone" was an open examination of the band's struggles with drug usage. It was a memorable tune on Appetite for Destruction because of its dark humor and catchy rhythm, and it demonstrated Izzy's ability to approach difficult issues with an unwavering honesty that was both engaging and disarming.

Izzy's songwriting contributed to the band's sound in more subtle yet no less significant ways than the band's major singles. His talent at crafting chord progressions and riffs served as the foundation for many of their tunes. His rhythm guitar playing, which is sometimes disregarded in favor of Slash's solos, was a major contributor to the dynamic energy of the band. Izzy had a minimalist approach on the guitar, emphasizing feel and rhythm above technical flair. In contrast to the elaborately manufactured rock that dominated the charts at the time, the band's music had a raw, organic sound because of this restraint.

Izzy's special talents went beyond just his musical prowess; he also served as the band's pillar of support. Izzy kept a modest profile while the other members frequently courted trouble with their outrageous acts and exaggerated egos. He was renowned for his diligence and concentration, which enabled the band to continue producing music even during its most turbulent times. He was a vital member of the group because of this sense of balance, especially throughout the rigorous writing and recording sessions for their first album and follow-up releases.

Izzy's flexibility as a songwriter was further demonstrated by hits like

"Patience," one of the outstanding songs from G N' R Lies. The band's typical hard-edged sound was broken up by the acoustic ballad's poignant lyrics and soft melody. The song was heavily influenced by Izzy, both in terms of its melancholy tone and its simple arrangement. It demonstrated that Guns N' Roses could be just as strong at quiet vulnerable times as they were in full-throttle rock mode, demonstrating his capacity for innovation and adaptation.

Izzy's ability to incorporate a variety of musical influences into the band's style was another important part of his talents. His passion for classic rock, blues, and punk rock gave Guns N' Roses a depth and variety that appealed to a wide range of listeners. Songs like "You Could Be Mine" and "Dust N' Bones," which combined elements of gritty narrative, swaggering rock, and raw passion, were especially notable examples of this eclecticism. Izzy was able to combine these inspirations to produce a sound that was both classic and distinctively their own.

Izzy was essential to the band's success, yet he never sought attention. His modesty, which contributed to his appeal, was his preference to let the music speak for itself. As the driving force behind Guns N' Roses' creative output, fans praised his sincerity and straightforward demeanor. Izzy stuck to his origins, concentrating on the art of songwriting rather than the distractions of popularity, even as the band's renown soared and the demands of success increased.

Izzy Stradlin made incalculable contributions to Guns N' Roses. His work with Axl Rose and the rest of the band as a key songwriter resulted in songs that shaped a time period and served as an inspiration to innumerable performers. His unique rhythm guitar approach and ability to combine unadulterated emotion with catchy melodies influenced the band's sound and legacy. Despite his frequent avoidance of the spotlight, Izzy's impact could be heard in every word and note, solidifying his place among rock's most recognizable and timeless personalities. His work with Guns N' Roses is proof of the strength of teamwork, genuineness, and the unwavering spirit of rock & roll.

Chapter 5

The Era of Guns N' Roses

Izzy Stradlin's time with Guns N' Roses was a time of ground-breaking innovation, international renown, and inner conflict; it embodied the pinnacles of rock success as well as the toll it could have on its inhabitants. As one of the original members, Izzy was essential to the band's success as a key composer whose musical intuition helped establish their style as well as a rhythm guitarist. Great artistic accomplishments, such as the explosive popularity of their first album and the ambitious scope of their subsequent works, characterized the Guns N' Roses era, but it was also teeming with difficulties that would ultimately result in Izzy's resignation.

The rock music scene was drastically altered in 1987 when Guns N' Roses released Appetite for Destruction. Fans disenchanted with the glossy glam rock that had dominated the decade found resonance in the album's raw energy, unpolished edge, and rebellious attitude, which encapsulated the mood of the late 1980s. This achievement was largely due to Izzy's subtle but important efforts. While his lyrics helped express the band's unvarnished and unrefined voice, his rhythm guitar skills served as a strong basis for Slash's explosive solos.

Guns N' Roses went from being a struggling band performing bars in Los Angeles to one of the biggest groups in the world when the unexpected and overwhelming success of Appetite for Destruction catapulted them into the spotlight. This quick ascent to fame was both thrilling and difficult for Izzy. The band's modest origins stood in sharp contrast to the demands of fame, media attention, and continual traveling. Even while the band relished their success, the constant pace and way of life started to wear them down. Being more of a reclusive and reflective person, Izzy frequently found himself at odds with the excesses that came to characterize the band's public persona.

Izzy's contribution as a songwriter remained crucial to Guns N' Roses' development as they moved from Appetite for Destruction to their next big endeavor. Released in 1991, the double album Use Your Illusion I & II demonstrated a more ambitious approach to their art and a wider range of musical styles. The band's development as musicians was reflected in the albums' blend of bluesy ballads, grandiose compositions, and hard-hitting rock choruses. This change was mostly due to Izzy's input. tracks like "Dust N' Bones," "You Ain't the First," and "Double Talkin' Jive" exhibited his unique approach, which was marked by unvarnished honesty and a minimalist look that stood in stark contrast to the more ornate production of other tracks on the albums.

Use Your Illusion I & II was a huge project that involved both internal conflicts and creative breakthroughs. Different perspectives and personalities started to collide as the band's prominence grew, leading to both artistic and personal disputes. Having always favored a simple, uncomplicated approach to music, Izzy frequently found himself at conflict with the band's increasingly complex direction. He further separated himself from the mayhem that surrounded the band with his dedication to sobriety, which he embraced after a turbulent time of substance misuse. Izzy wanted stability and focus, putting his health and artistic integrity first, while other members persisted in enjoying the excesses of celebrity.

Following the records' release, the band embarked on one of the most ambitious and taxing tours in rock history, called Use Your Illusion, which took them all over the world for over two years. The band's worldwide appeal was demonstrated by the tour, which drew sizable audiences and cemented their place among the greatest performers of the day. But it also made the group's divisions clear. Existing tensions were made worse by the unrelenting schedule and the demands of performing at such a high level. The tour turned out to be a pivotal moment for Izzy. His wish for a more controlled and grounded approach was completely at odds with the chaotic atmosphere, which was characterized by delays, arguments, and unpredictable conduct.

It was evident that Guns N' Roses' dynamics had changed by the time the Use Your Illusion era peaked. In addition to providing them with previously unheard-of chances, the band's meteoric popularity had also produced a volatile environment that was getting harder to control. Izzy eventually found the strain of life on the road, personal disputes, and artistic differences to be intolerable. He wanted to take back control of his life and artistic direction, which led him to decide to quit the band in 1991 for both personal and professional reasons.

An era for Guns N' Roses came to an end with Izzy Stradlin's departure. He made incalculable contributions to the band throughout his tenure, influencing its sound and legacy in ways that are still relevant today. As a guitarist, his calm presence served as a counterpoint to the band's exaggerated personas, and as a songwriter, he was unparalleled in his ability to transform raw emotion into powerful music. With all of its successes and setbacks, Izzy's career's Guns N' Roses period is still regarded as a pivotal period that cemented his status as a rock star and brought to light the difficulties of being a member of one of the greatest bands ever.

Chapter 6

The Departure

In 1991, Izzy Stradlin left Guns N' Roses, shocking both the music business and fans. It seemed unimaginable that a founding member would leave the band at the height of their popularity, when Use Your Illusion I & II was topping the charts and their world tour was in full force. But for Izzy, the choice was not only required, but also unavoidable. His reasons for leaving, how it affected the band and him, and the life he built thereafter all show how devoted he was to his beliefs and his work.

As the band's popularity soared, the atmosphere within Guns N' Roses became more and more tumultuous. There was little time for personal stability due to the demanding pace of media commitments, recording, and touring. The revelry that surrounded the band served as a sharp reminder of a life that Izzy had resolved to abandon after years of substance addiction. Izzy tried to stay focused and disciplined while the other members were going overboard. An increasing amount of frustration was caused by the difference in lifestyles. He frequently felt alone in the band, a sensation that was made worse by the internal strife that afflicted the group and the growing demands of their popularity.

Izzy's choice to quit was also significantly influenced by creative disagreements. With more intricate shows and a move toward opulent musical arrangements, Guns N' Roses had grown into a legendary band. This development ran counter to Izzy's goal, as his songwriting and musicianship were grounded in unadulterated passion and simplicity. He favored a more straightforward strategy that put honesty ahead of show. Izzy's discontent increased as the band's music evolved and the dynamics among the members got increasingly acrimonious. He became aware that the band's new orientation did not fit with his creative ideals.

The Use Your Illusion tour, a demanding two-year journey that pushed the band's unity to its breaking point, was the pivotal moment. The group's tensions were further exacerbated by the tour's numerous delays, onstage tantrums, and unpredictable environment. Izzy became quite irritated with some of her bandmates' unpredictable actions, especially Axl Rose. Izzy needed stability and wanted to concentrate on the music, but the unreliable and continual turmoil got in the way. Izzy formally quit Guns N' Roses in November 1991, not long after the Use Your Illusion CDs were released.

Izzy's exit had a significant effect on the band as well as on himself. Guns N' Roses lost a vital creative force and one of its most dependable and grounded members. The band's sound had relied heavily on Izzy's songwriting and rhythm guitar skills, thus it was challenging to replace the hole created by his departure. The group's chemistry irrevocably changed, although the remaining members continued to have economic success. The band's growing disarray, which would ultimately result in more departures and an extended period of inactivity, was exacerbated by the loss of Izzy's calming influence.

Izzy saw quitting Guns N' Roses as a chance to take back control of his life and go out on his own terms. He released his debut album, Izzy Stradlin and the Ju Ju Hounds, in 1992, concentrating on his solo career after being released from the band's disagreements and pressures. His passion for simple rock & roll was evident in the record, which combined punk, reggae, and blues components with an unadulterated, raw intensity. It was a sharp contrast to the opulence of Guns N' Roses' later work and a return to the straightforward simplicity that had always characterized Izzy's sound. The album garnered positive reviews from reviewers and fans, reinforcing Izzy's reputation as a gifted and genuine performer, even if it didn't have the same degree of economic success as Guns N' Roses.

Izzy mostly avoided the limelight in the years after his departure. He chose to live a more sedate, private life away from the extravagance and attention of his Guns N' Roses days. This choice was consistent with his nature; even at the height of the band's popularity, Izzy was renowned for his reserved manner and penchant for avoiding the spotlight. He was able to concentrate on what was most important to him—his music and his own health—by taking a break.

Izzy, who frequently recorded and released music on her own, kept putting out solo albums throughout the 1990s and 2000s. He was able to circumvent the limitations of the conventional music industry and retain total creative freedom thanks to this strategy. His solo work stayed faithful to his creative vision even though it was less well-known than Guns N' Roses' enormous popularity. His music's genuineness and honesty, which contrasted with the overly manufactured fads of the time, won numerous fans.

Izzy was also able to rediscover the things that made him happy and fulfilled in his life away from the limelight. He traveled, indulged in his love of motorbikes, and relished the independence that comes with escaping the pressures of celebrity. He remained friendly with his old bandmates even after leaving Guns N' Roses, sometimes getting back together for special appearances and joint ventures. Even though they were few, these occasions served as a reminder of his enduring influence on the band and their common past.

Izzy Stradlin's decision to leave Guns N' Roses was daring and out of the ordinary, but it demonstrated his steadfast devotion to his beliefs and his craft. He prioritized his personal well-being and creative independence over compromise by leaving the band at the height of its popularity. His choice had a long-lasting effect on his life and the band he helped create, solidifying his reputation as a musician who remained loyal to himself in a field that is sometimes characterized by excess and uniformity. The power of understanding when to take a step back, accept change, and create a path that is in line with one's principles and interests is demonstrated by Izzy's journey following Guns N' Roses.

Chapter 7

Izzy Stradlin and the Ju Ju Hounds

Izzy Stradlin looked for a new musical path after departing Guns N' Roses at the height of their popularity. This path would allow him to develop his own creative voice free from the turmoil and constraints of the mainstream rock industry. He made a major break from his work with Guns N' Roses in 1992 when he founded Izzy Stradlin and the Ju Ju Hounds. With a sound that included elements of classic rock, punk, and blues, the new band gave him the opportunity to go back to his origins in rock & roll. In 1992, the Ju Ju Hounds published their self-titled first album, which was a tribute to Izzy's idea of a more raw, stripped-down musical approach.

An important turning point in Izzy Stradlin's career was the creation of the

Ju Ju Hounds. He surrounded himself with musicians that shared his passion for simple, unadorned rock music after leaving behind the legendary presence of Guns N' Roses. Notable musicians including former Rolling Stones guitarist Rick Richards and bassist Jimmy Ashhurst were on the Ju Ju Hounds' roster. Izzy was able to rediscover the music that first influenced him through this new partnership, especially the gritty, loose vibe of rock from the late 1960s and early 1970s. The lavish staging and opulent arrangements that characterized a large portion of his earlier work with Guns N' Roses were removed from the album. Rather, it was an unvarnished, honest, and personal representation of Izzy's lyrics.

Izzy Stradlin and the Ju Ju Hounds' sound was influenced by a variety of musical styles, including classic rock, punk, and blues. Izzy's passion for the simplicity and vigor of the early rock and roll era was evident in songs like "Shuffle It All" and "Somebody Knockin'." In contrast to Guns N' Roses' more polished sound, there was a noticeable feeling of freedom in the music. The CD was charming despite its lack of refinement. It perfectly encapsulated the spirit of a musician withdrawing from the limelight and seeking comfort in the music instead of the spectacle or image that had surrounded his former band. Although the album didn't reach the same level of monetary success as his earlier efforts, it was nonetheless a critical hit. Nevertheless, it attracted a devoted following and confirmed Izzy's standing as a gifted and genuine rock songwriter.

The Ju Ju Hounds' music was distinguished by its rhythm and simplicity. Izzy's guitar playing was at the heart of the band's bluesy riffs and driving rhythms. In sharp contrast to Guns N' Roses' flamboyant intensity, his voice also had a more calm, easygoing tone. Izzy was able to explore a different aspect of his musical personality with this new path, one that was less centered on the extravagant reputation he had developed with Guns N' Roses and more on the origins of rock & roll. This change was also reflected in his lyrics. The Ju Ju Hounds' songs were more contemplative, frequently concentrating on relationships, personal challenges, and the small joys in life, in contrast to his prior work, which frequently dealt with themes of excess, rebellion, and turmoil.

Despite not enjoying the same level of popularity as Guns N' Roses, the Ju Ju Hounds had a significant influence on rock music, especially in the alternative and roots rock genres. In some respects, their sound was ahead of its time, foreshadowing the emergence of more guitar-driven, minimalist rock bands in the late 1990s and early

2000s. Fans who were tired of the overly manufactured and polished sound of popular music were drawn to the album's unpolished, raw vibe and dedication to simple rock & roll. The Ju Ju Hounds' honesty and hard work won them a devoted fan base among people who valued their straightforward approach to rock music, despite the fact that they did not top the charts as Guns N' Roses did.

Even though it didn't do well commercially, Izzy Stradlin and the Ju Ju Hounds' legacy is nevertheless important when considering Izzy's career. Without the limitations of his previous band, it signified a return to his origins and a reimagining of his musical identity. It also gave him a creative avenue to experiment with the sound and aesthetic that had always spoken to him the most. Izzy was able to be himself as a person and as a musician thanks to the Ju Ju Hounds. He was just doing the music he wanted to produce, free from the demands of the music business, and wasn't pursuing the notoriety or renown that had come with Guns N' Roses.

The Ju Ju Hounds toured in support of the album's release, but the endeavor didn't last long. After the band's roster changed, Izzy ultimately went on to pursue other solo endeavors while still putting out songs under his own name. The Ju Ju Hounds, however, continued to be a pivotal point in his career. Izzy's wish to abandon the flash and glamour of the mainstream rock scene and get back to the simplicity and genuineness that had always been at the heart of his musical expression was mirrored by the record and the band.

Even though Izzy Stradlin and the Ju Ju Hounds didn't achieve the same level of success as Guns N' Roses, the project gave Izzy the chance to establish his own musical identity and choose a route that was more in line with his creative vision and personal beliefs. The band's honest and unvarnished sound encapsulated the essence of an artist regaining his creative independence and escaping the demands of celebrity. Despite their brief existence, the Ju Ju Hounds' influence on Izzy's career and their role in the development of rock music continue to be significant aspects of his musical development.

Chapter 8

Solo Career and Reinvention

Following his split from Guns N' Roses in 1991, Izzy Stradlin entered a new phase of artistic freedom characterized by his independence and wanting to break away from the excesses of the mainstream music business. He released a number of solo albums that were frequently subdued, self-produced, and intensely personal, allowing him to develop his own musical voice free from the demands of fame and expectations. Izzy's solo career turned into a reinvention trip where he could work with other musicians, explore with new sounds, and hone his musical approach while still having the freedom he had always desired.

Compared to his time with Guns N' Roses, Izzy took a very different approach to his solo career. Without the support of large companies and sometimes with little fanfare, he issued his independent albums on his own terms. His aim to keep things uncomplicated, unpolished, and authentic was mirrored in his do-it-yourself attitude. Izzy Stradlin and the Ju Ju Hounds, his 1992 debut solo album, was a perfect example of this philosophy. The album received critical acclaim for its simple and basic rock & roll sound, while not being a major financial success. It offered a more natural and unadorned manner that appealed to fans who valued Izzy's genuineness, in contrast to Guns N' Roses' refined and ornate production.

Izzy Stradlin continued to make solo music in a similar style after the release of Izzy Stradlin and the Ju Ju Hounds, albeit the production became more and more simple. He took a more minimalist approach to his music with his second album, *117°, which came out in 1998. It combined parts of Americana, blues, and rock with the same unadulterated fire that had characterized his previous work. His dedication to artistic independence was once again demonstrated by the album's independent release. The album was highly welcomed by critics and fans who appreciated its authentic, straightforward approach to rock music, despite the fact that it was not a monetary success. The album's title, 117°, further emphasized the contemplative and intimate tone of the music by referencing the temperature in the California desert hamlet where Izzy wrote and recorded a large portion of the album.

Although it had a somewhat more polished sound, Izzy's 2000 solo album Ride the Night continued to explore the same musical ground as his earlier albums. The record, which combined elements of country, rock, and blues with a more modern production, demonstrated his developing musical style. Ride the Night, which was released independently like his previous work, demonstrated his ability to write catchy songs while maintaining his distinctive style. Izzy also experimented with a variety of musical styles on the album, which demonstrated his readiness to change and develop as a performer without sacrificing who he is.

Izzy's solo career was characterized by both his independent records and his joint ventures with other musicians. He was able to keep pushing the boundaries of his music while maintaining the unadulterated, natural sound that had come to define him via his collaborations with various musicians. Izzy worked with a number of musicians in the early 2000s, notably Duff McKagan, the former bassist for Guns N' Roses, who frequently joined Izzy on his solo endeavors. The two collaborated on songs that combined punk, blues, and hard rock elements, and their work together became a distinctive feature of Izzy's music after Guns N' Roses.

Even though Izzy preferred working alone, he was prepared to take center stage for a few special projects. His status as a well-respected and adaptable musician was further cemented by his guest performances on other musicians' albums. His former bandmates from Guns N' Roses were one of his most well-known partners. Over the years, Izzy occasionally performed with Guns N' Roses, including as a guest at special events and concerts. Though his engagement was always sporadic, his presence in these occasions allowed him to reconnect with Axl Rose and the other members of the band and reminded fans of his basic position in the band. Throughout his solo career, Izzy's musical approach changed, but the essence of his sound stayed the same: a punk, rock, and blues combination with a focus on authenticity and simplicity. He kept trying out different genres as the years passed, incorporating more Americana and country elements into his songs. This development reflected his increasing musical maturity as he attempted to combine new sound worlds with his heritage. However, he never completely gave up on the unadulterated, unrefined components that had first characterized his music. With songs that centered on themes of relationships, personal development, and time passing, his solo work was frequently personal and introspective.

Izzy had an unrelenting commitment to his solo career, and his self-reliant approach to music gave him a sense of creative freedom that many of his contemporaries did not. He escaped the traps of celebrity and the demands of the commercial music industry by putting out albums on his own terms and collaborating with a changing group of artists. His solo work was always intended to be an honest representation of his creative vision rather than to be a mass-market hit.

Izzy Stradlin's solo career is still an important part of his musical legacy even if it never saw the same degree of financial success as his time with Guns N' Roses. He has gained acclaim as a musician who remains loyal to himself because of his ability to carve out his own route and uphold his creative integrity in the face of the pull of popular popularity. Fans who respect his genuineness and dedication to making music according to his own terms continue to enjoy his solo effort. Izzy Stradlin showed that his genuine love is music, not the fame or wealth that accompanies it, through his independent recordings, changing musical style, and partnerships with other musicians.

Chapter 9

Life Beyond the Stage

Izzy Stradlin has a reputation for being mysterious and reclusive, particularly when it comes to his life off the stage. He has purposefully kept his personal life under wraps throughout his career in order to avoid the constant attention that comes with being famous. He has become somewhat of a mystery due to his desire for solitude, particularly in contrast to other Guns N' Roses members whose private lives were frequently made public. The exaggerated identities that came with his former band's stardom stand in stark contrast to Izzy's approach to fame and his relationships. He chose a more modest and independent life than the glamorous lifestyle of rock stars.

Izzy's private life has been characterized by a subtle rebellion on both a personal and professional level. He has seldom been forthcoming about his romances, sometimes opting to conceal information about his love life from the public. Izzy appreciates his privacy and has made an effort to keep a low profile, even if a lot of his personal background is still mostly unknown. Izzy favored maintaining a limited social circle and spending a significant portion of his time in relative solitude, in contrast to many of his peers who frequently adopted the rock and roll lifestyle of excess. He has been known to reside in more subdued, calmer neighborhoods throughout the years, frequently eschewing the glitz and glamour of celebrity that would have brought attention to his private life.

Izzy has always had a complicated relationship with celebrities. He gained a place in the rock canon because of his skill and contributions to Guns N' Roses, but he never seemed to want to embrace the celebrity culture that accompanied being a member of one of the largest bands in the world. He famously shied away from interviews and seldom ever sought attention. Izzy remained one of the most withdrawn members of Guns N' Roses, even during their most successful period. He avoided the usual rock star lifestyle, which frequently included excessive media attention, drinking, and the selfish pursuit of fame. Izzy was frequently direct and contemptuous of the industry's obsession with celebrity in interviews and public appearances, emphasizing that his main focus was always the music. Izzy saw music as a means of expression rather than a means of being well-known.

Despite being a member of a band that came to represent the excesses of the rock scene in the 1980s and early 1990s, Izzy had a more realistic view of fame and the music business. He frequently expressed his dissatisfaction with the music industry's contrived character, stating that it seemed cut off from the real creative process that initially drew him to music. Izzy was never one to participate in the fantasy of becoming a rock star, and his final resignation from Guns N' Roses was partly due to his contempt for the flimsy parts of celebrity. Due to the band's increasing financial success as well as the internal strife and struggle that accompanied its ascent, Izzy left the group in pursuit of a less hectic and more satisfying existence. He never saw success or celebrity as the motivation behind his music; rather, it was always about the craft.

His post-Guns N' Roses career reflected this sense of freedom. Izzy preferred independent endeavors above business endeavors and kept releasing music on his own terms after splitting from the band. He chose to release his songs more independently rather than through large labels, avoiding the usual path of a rock star. This choice was in line with his wish to have creative control and stay away from the glitz and glamour that had defined his early years with the band.

Izzy's choice to live away from the spotlight may be the clearest indication of his dislike for the rock star lifestyle. Because he prefers to stay away from interviews and public appearances, he has hardly been seen in the media. He has always had few encounters with the media and fans, and he has refrained from talking about his personal life in interviews. Despite his enormous success as a musician, he mostly avoided attention by declining to participate in the customary promotional cycles and events that would have kept him in the spotlight. Even when Guns N' Roses was performing or recording, he frequently avoided the spotlight due to his desire for privacy, choosing instead to concentrate on his own music rather than enjoy the notoriety that came with the band's success.

Izzy's romances have also mostly stayed under wraps. He has mostly kept his love relationships and family life out of the public glare, while there have been sporadic glimpses into his personal life, especially in regard to his time in Los Angeles. His general concept of keeping his personal and work lives apart is in line with this. Izzy has always kept his personal affairs quiet, preferring to let his music speak for itself, in contrast to many other superstars who have utilized their personal life to enhance their public image. His reticence to interact with the more surface-level aspects of celebrity has garnered him some respect from fans and industry insiders, who value his sense of solitude.

Izzy's impact on the music industry is indisputable, even if he prefers to keep his affairs private. His legacy is one of sincerity, independence, and creative integrity. His solo work and contributions to Guns N' Roses have had a lasting impact on rock music. Even though he avoided the limelight, his music still has an impact on people who appreciate unadulterated passion and honesty in their work. Izzy's goal in life off of the stage has been to preserve his integrity and sense of self, even if it means eschewing the fame and notoriety that many rock musicians long for. In this sense, Izzy Stradlin continues to be one of the most fascinating and well-respected individuals in rock history—a performer who keeps his private life well hidden and lets his music speak for itself.

www.ingramcontent.com/pod-product-compliance
Ingram Content Group UK Ltd.
Pitfield, Milton Keynes, MK11 3LW, UK
UKHW020701270825
7594UKWH00039B/892

9 798309 592289